"Why Am I Here?"
Understanding Why I am in State Foster Care

Theresa Greenlee-Jeffers
Author and Illustrator

Earthly Stories with a Heavenly Meaning

"Why Am I Here?"
Understanding Why I am in State Foster Care
Theresa Greenlee-Jeffers
Author and Illustrator

Copyright @ Theresa Greenlee-Jeffers

February 2018

All Rights Reserved. No part of this book may be reproduced or utilized in any form or by any means, electronic or mechanical, including photocopying, recording, or by any information storage and retrieval system, without permission in writing from the author.

ISBN 978-1-945698-44-6
Printed in the United States of America

Readers should be aware that Internet Web sites offered as citations and/or sources for further information may have been changed or disappeared between the time this was written and when it is read.

"Why Am I Here?"
Understanding Why I am in State Foster Care

Theresa Greenlee-Jeffers
Author and Illustrator

PUBLISHED by
PARABLES
Earthly Stories with a Heavenly Meaning

Dedicated to "Austin"

...your fear and confusion of why it happened to you gave me inspiration to write this book.

I pray that the words and explanations would bring comfort to others,

just like it did to you!

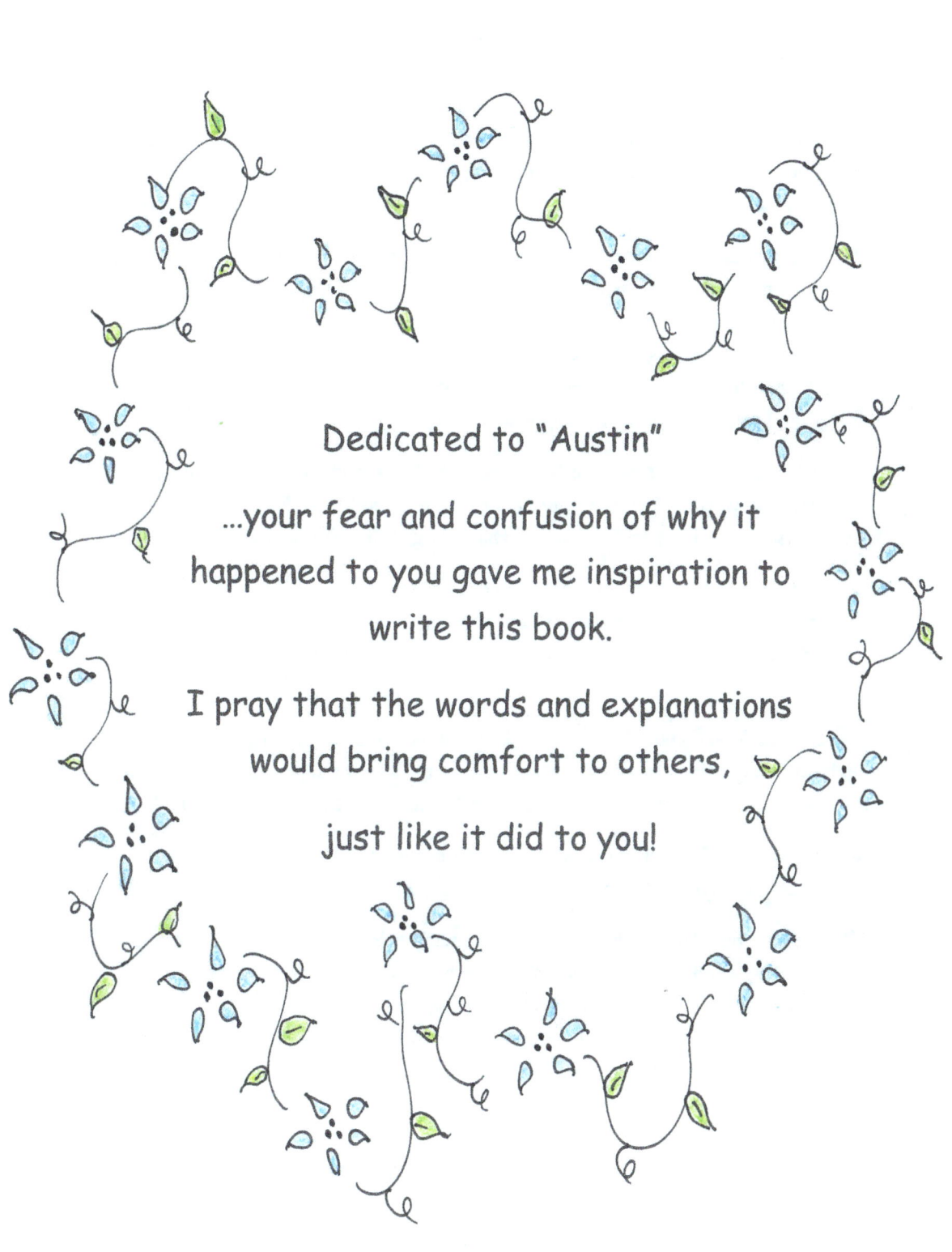

FOREWARD

I remember times when I thought my life was over, that is was not worth living I thought I could not recover from the things that had happened. Random cruel things in my life hurt me – abuse, rejection, sickness. I did not see love or God –none of the things those nice people talked about to make me feel better.

The thing about life, especially with God, is that your story does not have to end with pain. There is much MUCH more good things after this pain. Your abuse, your sickness, your rejection, it may stay with you or it may go away. I am telling you that your pain CAN be healed, even transformed into something that helps others. It sounds crazy, impossible even, I know, but it is true. I have lived this truth over and over again.

Many times, I thought my life had a period at the endpoint of my pain, but it was not the stopping point, it was a comma, a pause, not the end. Either my pain passed or I learned how to use the pain and the pause was over.

I do not know the end of my story. Pain was not the end, it was just a part of the story. I could make my story about more than suffering. I could let God use my pain for something beautiful, like counseling children. This is exactly what He did for ME.

My pain made me what I am today. It made me weaker, stronger, and more understanding. My pain made me want to help hurting people. My pain helped me believe in God who is our Father, our Healer, our Sacrifice, and our Friend.

I still wish some of my childhood had not happened and I wish that I had never caused anyone else suffering, but that is not the way life works.

YOUR story beautiful children who are reading this, is not just about the pain you have experienced. You may have gone through things that you thought would never end. These things that happened to you were NOT your fault – you did NOT ask for it to happen. You may have been hurt sexually, physically, emotionally. You may have been starved, ignored, spit on, touched or hurt in places that make you never want to be touched again. All of this happened, it is real hurt and pain. People may have hurt you more when you asked for help. It might be that you feel and think that no one loves you. Maybe to you, love equals pain. You may even feel that God left you or that God was never there.

My beautiful children, this is NOT THE END. Pain CAN be healed. God hears your cries and sees your tears, even the ones you cry in the dark – the ones that you cannot cry because it hurts too much. What you went through is not the end of your story. God has so much more in mind for you. You are beautiful children of a loving God who NEVER wanted any of this to happen to you. God loves you. God is with you. God's love is NEVER hurtful. God has NEVER left you, even when it felt like you were alone in the dark.

The abuse you went through and the horrible pain is the reason my dear friend wrote this book. God is reaching out to you through her books to soothe your hearts, your minds and your dear spirits. My friend wants you to know that you are beautiful and you are loved; and if you do not know this yet because you were hurt, this is not the end of your story.

You did not have choices before, but you are beginning to have choices now. The story can get better and you can be free of this hurt and pain. God can do this in a way beyond anything you or I can ever imagine.

The story of your life is not over. You can be free from this pain, or the pain can stay with you. If the pain never goes away fully you can use it to help others. How you use your story is YOUR CHOICE.

May God bless you and may God heal you as you walk with Him throughout your precious life.

Therese

Julie Kringas Johnson, LPC-S

My name is Jacob, I am 7 years old. I have a baby brother named Austin. Austin is 3 years old. Me and my brother are sad and scared just like you are right now. We are sad because we cannot live at OUR house right now. We are scared because we do not know the people we are staying with tonight. We had, NO CHOICE!

My Mom and Dad were making BAD CHOICES. Because they were making BAD CHOICES they were not taking care of me and my brother. People came to our house and moved us away from our home to help keep us safe. Miss Andrea is the lady that held my hand and she buckled me and my brother into the car. Miss Andrea works for Child Protective Services.

The people we are staying with, Miss Kathy and Mr. Jeff are very nice to us. We even ate dinner with them and their kids at a kitchen table. Miss Kathy asked what me and Austin's favorite thing to eat is and we said mac & cheese! Miss Kathy gave us a CHOICE and we ate mac & cheese!

When we left home today I did not get any of my clothes, not even my favorite thing in the whole world to sleep with, my monkey! Miss Kathy went to the store and bought me and Austin some clothes to sleep in and play in, but I never told her about my monkey that I like to sleep with. I miss my monkey!

It is now morning time. Miss Kathy rocked my baby brother Austin all night because he was crying. He misses our Mommy. I do not let them see me cry. We are scared we will never see our Mommy and Daddy ever again! Will they ever make GOOD CHOICES? I am so angry at my Mommy and Daddy! Do they even love us?

The nice lady from Child Protective Services, Miss Andrea came to see us today. She took us shopping for more clothes and even bought us a toy!
Miss Andrea told us her job is to make sure that me and Austin are safe until my parents learn how to make better choices so THEY can take care of us.

I told Miss Andrea that I take real good care of me and Austin. I always make sure he eats and brushes his teeth. Miss Andrea said she knew I was doing a good job, but it is my PARENTS responsibility to take care of US. She said it may take them a little while to learn how to make GOOD CHOICES. Until our Mom and Dad can make GOOD CHOICES, WE have to live someplace else! WE HAVE NO CHOICE!

It just does not seem fair! My Mom and Dad made BAD CHOICES, not me! Why are me and Austin the ones that have to be punished! We had to leave our house, our toys, our friends and even our school to stay with strangers!! It is NOT FAIR, I HAVE NO CHOICE!

I am ANGRY, I WANT TO GO HOME!
Do my parents even care that I am staying with STRANGERS? Do they miss me and Austin? What happens if they NEVER make GOOD CHOICES?

I am angry at my parents!
Mr. Jeff told me that being angry at my parents BAD CHOICES is okay.
He explained that everyone needs help learning how to make GOOD CHOICES.
Some people, even grown-ups need more time to learn HOW to make GOOD
CHOICES. I still have NO CHOICE!

Miss Kathy and Mr. Jeff told me and Austin that they will be our Foster Parents while we live with them. We will be their Foster Children. They promise to take care of us and be responsible for us until my parents can. I like them very much, but I still have NO CHOICE!

Today is the day when the Judge will decide if me and Austin can go back home to live. The Judge will listen to all of the grown-ups that have talked to me and Austin. As a "Foster" kid you get to talk to A LOT of different grown-ups. We have talked to our "Worker", Miss Andrea and Mrs. Jones our counselor. You might even get to talk to a therapist, or talk to some doctors. You might even talk to a policeman or police lady. The Judge, the lawyers and our parents meet together to talk about things. Sometimes, the Judge will have your parents take classes or maybe see a counselor, or maybe a doctor. Miss Kathy said we are lucky because so many adults want to make sure we are taken care of. I did not know so many grown-ups cared about us.

I did not know what the Judge will decide today. I do not know if we will be able to go home. I hope my parents are learning how to make GOOD Choices. I love my parents but I am very angry and hurt. Mrs. Jones, our counselor, said that my feelings are "normal" feelings and it is ok to be angry and to be hurt.

She said she was very glad to know I love my parents. She said that when we love someone we ALWAYS love them, even if we are angry or hurt.

Mrs. Jones said I should write my feelings on a sheet of paper, or even draw a picture of how I am feeling. She said I can give the paper to my Mom when I see her. My feelings paper will help me tell her how I feel about her BAD CHOICES and how her choices hurt my feelings. I REALLY LIKE that I idea!

I made my "FEELINGS" paper! Austin made a "FEELINGS" paper too. I have a lot of different feelings on my paper. I have shared some paper in this book so you can make your own "FEELINGS" paper. You might have different feelings than me. Whatever you feel is ok, those are YOUR feelings. Mrs. Jones, my counselor told me that I can tell my Mom and Dad how I feel, but I need to remember they have feelings too. I am learning how to share my feelings. Mrs. Jones said that it is important to learn how to communicate the right way. Miss Kathy and Mr. Jeff help us share our feelings in their home. I think that is pretty cool!

Our story is not over yet. I wish we could go home now but my parents have more work to do. The good thing about my foster parents is that they are teaching us how to communicate the right way. We are learning things to help us be good parents one day.

I have no idea how my story will work out. I hope that my parents learn how to make GOOD CHOICES.
The only thing I know for sure is that Miss Kathy and Mr. Jeff are really nice Foster Parents. They take real good care of me and Austin. If I cannot live at my house I am glad I can stay here, at least for now.

Can you find yourself? These are Foster Kids!

What about YOUR story? Where are you at in YOUR story? Is this your first day in Foster Care? Have you been in Foster Care for a long time?
Is this your first Foster home? Your second Foster home? I know that like me, you have A LOT of feelings about being in Foster Care. Would you like to share how you are feeling about being in Foster Care?

Would you like to make a "FEELINGS" paper like me and Austin made? It is easy to do. You can use words or you can draw pictures of how you are feeling.

I like making the "Feeling Faces" that my Counselor, Mrs. Jones shared with me. I drew some of the "Feeling Faces" on this page so you can use them if you want to.

The next few pages in this book were made for you to share YOUR Feelings.

Things I want to remember about my time in Foster Care:

The day I came into foster care was _____.

The city I live in is called _____.

I live with _____
_____.

My Child Protective Services Worker is _____
_____.

When do I visit with my biological family? _____
_____
_____.

Do my Foster Parents have pets? _____ Yes or _____ No

What kind of pets do they have? _____.

What are the names of their pets? _____.

Do my Foster Parents have other children? _____ Yes or _____ No

What are the names of the other children? _____
_____,
_____.

What do I like about being at my Foster Parents home? _____
_____,
_____.

My FEELINGS Page:
How I feel about everything that is happening around me.

My FEELINGS Page:
What I think about being in Foster Care

I wish I could tell you that I know what will happen for you, but I have no idea what will happen for you or for me!
The hardest part for me, is knowing that I have NO CHOICE in what is happening around me.
Mr. Jeff and Miss Kathy remind me that I can only control how I REACT to the things happening around me; I can make GOOD CHOICES or I can make BAD CHOICES. It is my decision!
Which choice will you make GOOD choices or BAD choices?

Glossary

<u>NO CHOICE</u> - taking the power of choosing away.

<u>BAD CHOICES</u> - decisions that are not healthy or wise or safe for that person or persons in their care.

<u>Child Protective Services (CPS)</u> - agency that is responsible for providing child protection, includes responding to reports of child abuse or neglect. CPS is also known by the name of "Department of Social Services" (DSS), "Social Services" and "Department of Children and Family Services" (DCFS).

<u>Consequences</u> - something not good that follows a bad choice, bad action or poor decision.

<u>CHOICE</u> - the act of choosing, the power of choosing, making your own decision.

<u>LOVE</u> - deep concern for someone, commitment to care for someone; to feel passion or strong affection for someone or something.

<u>GOOD CHOICES</u> - decisions/actions that are healthy, wise and safe for oneself and for those within their care.

<u>Responsibility</u> - being accountable for something or someone that you are taking care of; doing what is best for the other person.

Glossary

State (Agency) Case Worker – person assigned to work with or for someone to help a situation improve or change; they help keep children and adults safe from harm; and help to improve the lives of family members.

Punished – to subject to pain, loss, or confinement as a penalty for some offense or fault.

Angry – feeling or emotion of strong resentment.

Strangers – person(s) with whom one has no personal acquaintance, unknown to each other.

NEVER – not ever, absolutely not, not at all.

Foster Parents – person (family) that cares for a child who is not his or her biological child.

Biological – related to a family by blood, related by birth, genetically related.

Foster Child – a child placed into a group home or private home of a state certified caregiver.

Therapist/Counselor – a person trained in a particular kind of therapy treatment to help others.

Case – information about a particular situation, or person(s); incident, problem or event(s) associated with the situation at hand.

Glossary

Judge – public official authorized to decide on cases brought before the court.

Lawyer – person who is professionally trained in and practices law.

Police Officer – person whose job is to enforce laws, investigate crimes, make arrests, and to help keep citizens safe.

Doctor – person trained and who practices medicine; helps restore health through diagnosis, and treatment of disease, injury or any another physical or mental impairment.

Feelings – to form an opinion based upon emotion.

Foster Care – the State or Government system where a minor child or teen has been placed into an Orphanage, a Group Home, or in the home of a State-Certified Caregiver(s), referred to as "Foster Parent(s)"; or placed with a biological family member that has been approved by the State. The placement of the child is typically arranged by the State or the Social Service Agency of the State, whose job is to assist individuals and families during difficult times.

A Word of Encouragement and Advice from Miss Andrea

As a former Child Welfare Specialist for the State of Louisiana, I have worked many foster care cases. Many of my cases resulted in great outcomes for the safety of the children involved. The cases that had the best outcomes were the cases in which the whole team of people involved worked together. The team may include, but is not limited to, the Case Manager, the Foster Parents, the Biological Parents and any provider or specialist that works for the child's safety and best interest. I strongly believe that the child should be viewed as one of the most valuable team members. To be more specific, that child should have access to as much information about his or her situation in foster care as available. There are a lot of unknowns involved, but the more children can know what to expect the easier the process is for them to handle. The information about their family situation should be explained in age-appropriate language that the child understands. This book demonstrates a simplified, age-appropriate guide for children who must endure the stressors of entering the foster care system.

To the child or youth reading this, know first and foremost, that this situation is not your fault! You have to endure the foster care system because of the actions taken by those who are supposed to keep you safe.

The foster parents taking care of you want you to feel safe while your biological parents or guardians learn ways to make better decisions and take actions to better care for you. The hope is if your parents do what they need to in order to keep you safe, then you will return back to them. If your parent/s cannot learn how to keep you safe, your foster family will help you get through this experience by showing you love and taking care of you for as long as needed or until you find a permanent family through adoption or guardianship.

To the foster/adoptive parents reading this, you are this child's life line right now. Please use compassion and understanding while this child is placed in your home. Children have reported feeling angry, scared, confused and sad when they are going through foster care. Please be aware that children have a hard time expressing their feelings and may act out as a way to cope with what they are feeling inside. You are the hero, but you may be interpreted as the enemy by the child initially. Try not to take the child's behavior personally. The child just wants to be heard and treated well. Encourage the child by not talking negatively about his/her biological parents. Work as a team with the biological parents for the best interest of the child.

When the child feels like there are multiple people on the same page that love them, their experience in foster care is much easier. Please lean on the foster care worker for support when you need it.

Being a foster/adoptive parent can be very challenging, but know that with your compassion and understanding that you could be the only consistently positive role model in this child's life. You can make a significant difference in the life of the child in your care.

To the biological parent/s reading this, do not be discouraged. Use this situation as motivation to get your child/children back and your life back. Work your case plan. Make the foster parents and the foster care worker your ally for the benefit of your child. Show the system that even though you got it wrong the first time that you will do whatever it takes to correct your mistakes and learn how to be a better parent. If you cannot, or will not, do what you need to do to achieve a safe environment for your child, be straight forward with the foster care worker so that they can try to find a permanent, loving family that will keep your child safe and help your child/children thrive.

My best to you all,
Andrea Allen
a.k.a. "Miss Andrea"

RESOURCES:

As a Foster Parent, you can always reach out to your Home Developer when you have questions about your placement. Your Home Developer wants your placement to be positive for not only you, but for the child(ren) in your care. You also have the child's worker in your corner. Their desire is for the child(ren) to have an easy adjustment into your home, no matter how long they are there with you.

If you find that you have a need for more information or support during what can be a challenging process, you will find a list of various resources you can reach out to.

Being a Foster Parent is NOT for the weak of heart. YOU are an integral partner in this family's life. Yes I said, FAMILY. You are the part of the TEAM that provides, not only, shelter, but you provide the nurturing, mentoring and guidance the child(ren) placed in your home needs at this time in their life. THAT can be an overwhelming thought. The good news is you are not alone! There are other Foster Parents that can give you advice and guidance and encouragement.

Here are a few resources to assist you:

(You will also find extra pages for you to write in your own resources, those that you may find are specific for your area.)

- *National Foster Parent Association* www.nfpaonline.org/fplinks
  NFPA – WONDERFUL organization that truly cares about Foster Parents and the role they have.

- *Adopt US Kids* https://www.adoptuskids.org
  This site is not only for adoption, they give insight on your role as an Foster Parent and resources to help you be successful.

- *Child Welfare* (Government Agency) https://www.childwelfare.gov
  They offer a WEALTH of information on MANY various topics dealing with Child Welfare and families.

- *Administration for Children & Families* https://www.acf.hhs.gov
  They are a division of the Department of Health & Human Services.
- *Children's Bureau* under the *ACF* https://www.acf.hhs.gov/cb

- www.transitionschildrenservices.org
  559-222-5437   Email: info@transitionschildrenservices.org

- Monroe Harding, Nashville, TN https://www.monroeharding.org
  This organization has been assisting children for 125 years (at the printing of this book in 2018). They are a non-profit, tax exempt organization as classified under section 501©(3) of the Internal Revenue Code.
  You can like them on Facebook: Monroe Harding
  615-298-5573   Email: fostercare@monroeharding.org

- National Foster Care Coalition www.nationalfostercare.org
  Washington, DC Email: nationalfostercare@gmail.com $25 yearly membership

- The Annie E. Casey Foundation www.aecf.org
  Baltimore, MD 410-547-6600 *Wonderful organization that leads Workshops, has Community involvement and offers Webinars and a varied list of resources for Foster Parents, Child Welfare Workers and the children they serve.

- Raintree Services, Inc. in Louisiana 504-899-9045
  https://www.raintreeservices.org/program/raintree-family-fosterparent
  Email: info@raintreeservices.org
  You can follow Raintree on Facebook and on Twitter @RaintreeNOLA

- Serenity, Inc. Foster Care & Adoption in Southern California
  www.serenitykids.com   626-859-6200

- Crossroads NOLA, New Orleans, LA 504-482-9135
  This is a faith-based 501-c3 nonprofit organization committed to making a difference in the lives of children in foster care in New Orleans.

- Christian Alliance For Orphans, McLean, VA https://cafo.org
  When you visit their website you will find a wealth of helpful resources.

- Royal Family Kids, Santa Ana, CA   https://rfk.org
  714-438-2494   Email: office@royalfamilykids.org

- Backyard Orphans, Midlothian, TX www.backyardorphans.org

- Buckner Children and Family Services (and MANY more services offered)
  Dallas, TX 214-758-8023/855-264-8783 www.buckner.org

- ABBA FUND www.abbafund.org
  If funds are available, they can assist with no interest loans for adoption.

- Parent Center Hub   www.parentcenterhub.org
  Site gives great resources for Fostering and Adoptive Parents.

- American Academy of Pediatrics   1-866-843-2271
  https://www.aap.org/en-us/advocacy-and-policy

- Adoption Bridge, Newport Coast, CA Email: info@everychildhasaname.org
  (Every Child Has A Name)

- Kids Matter Inc.   https://www.kidsmatterinc.org
  414-344-1220   Email: adam@kidsmatterinc.org

- Lifesong for Orphans – The Forgotten Initiative, Gridley, IL
  https://theforgotteninitiative.org   309-747-4557

- iFoster Inc., Offices in California, Louisiana, New York
  www.ifoster.org   530-550-9645/855-936-7837

- CASA – Court Appointed Special Advocates (for Children)
  www.casaforchildren.org   EVERY child in foster care SHOULD have a CASA Worker…unfortunately, there are more children than there are CASA volunteers.

This is not all of the organizations and groups that offer training, support and encouragement for Foster Parents and Foster Children. You can search the words:
"Foster Parent" or "Foster Parenting" and a large number of groups and organizations will pop up on your screen. Each group offers varied information and you can seek the information you are looking for and find your answer amongst all of the sites.

You can also search your state's website for:
"How to become a foster parent". If you are unable to locate the information you are looking for there, you can call your local Department of Social Services Office for assistance.

As you take this journey, together, may each of you (Foster Child and Foster Parent) learn to work together for healing, trust and a better tomorrow.

A BIG heartfelt THANK YOU to the following:

First, THANK YOU Heavenly Father for the words you have given me to share. Father, without YOU, I am not sure where I would have ended up. Thank you Lord For loving me, even when I am not lovable. You have blest me beyond anything I Would have ever thought possible! I LOVE YOU my GRACIOUS HEAVENLY Father! Philippians 4:13

*James, my dear husband, thank you for your support! Thank you for eating too many "quick dinners" so I could get this work completed! Your love and prayers have encouraged me and lifted me up. Thank you for having faith in what the Lord has in store with me and for our family. I LOVE YOU JAMES!

*Gabbie and Carlos, ALL of this began because I fell in love with you BOTH! Thank you two for encouraging me, doing extra chores and for eating too many "quick dinners" with Daddy so I could work on this project. Thank you both for your valuable input and allowing me to draw from your own personal experiences to be able to reach others. You are both AWESOME! I am so pleased to see how the Lord is working in both of your lives, even at your young ages. I cannot wait to see what God has in store for the rest of your story! Remember... I LOVED YOU BOTH FIRST!

*"Miss Andrea"...it means so much that you agreed to write the Foreword for this book; not to mention being a "part" IN the book! You are an AWESOME Case Worker. Thank you for your encouragement and support in this project! I am grateful the Lord brought you into our life.

*Miss Julie, I cannot tell you how much your prayers, your encouragement and your confidence in how the Lord is at work through me has meant to me. I am so very THANKFUL to the Lord for bringing our lives together.

*Bro. John Jeffries...You are a TREMENDOUS BLESSING! I am ever so grateful to have been able to take this journey with YOU as my guide! Your wisdom and encouragement has meant more than you will ever know! I am THANKFUL for YOU and for, Published by Parables, for taking this leap of faith with me! I know the Lord has more in store for us both!

And last, but most certainly NOT least...

*ASAP Printing & Digital Imaging located in Slidell, Louisiana –
Ms. Marisa, Miss Heidi, and Mr. Micah... THANK YOU!!!
YOU guys are the BEST thing since sliced Bread!
Miss Heidi, the talent you have with taking an idea and making it into something BEAUTIFUL is a GIFT! The work you have done for the covers of my books are INCREDIBLE! Your design work is BETTER than I could have ever imagined! THANK YOU Miss Heidi for ALL of your hard work on these projects. HEIDI ROCKS!
Ms. Marisa and Mr. Micah, I cannot express my gratitude for having the privilege and opportunity to get to know you both.
I am HONORED to be able to work with your company, ASAP, not only with my books, but also with our family business, Datburnit Candles Incorporated. It gives me a peaceful feeling knowing I can call you with a "need" and it is taken care of! There are very few people that I KNOW I can depend on like that and you guys at ASAP Printing & Digital Imaging are at the VERY TOP!
I LOVE each one of you...and Buster too! ASAP is MY VIP!

Buster

www.ingramcontent.com/pod-product-compliance
Lightning Source LLC
Chambersburg PA
CBHW081357080526
44588CB00016B/2525